AF211667

SAAB JACKSON

MENTAL DISORDER

The Ultimate Guide to Mental Illness and Brain Disorders, Learn All the Important Information About Common Mental Illnesses and Disorders

Descrierea CIP a Bibliotecii Naționale a României
SAAB JACKSON
   MENTAL DISORDER. The Ultimate Guide to Mental Illness and Brain Disorders, Learn All the Important Information About Common Mental Illnesses and Disorders /
Saab Jackson. – Bucharest: Editura My Ebook, 2020
   ISBN

SAAB JACKSON

MENTAL DISORDER

The Ultimate Guide to Mental Illness and Brain Disorders,
Learn All the Important Information About Common
Mental Illnesses and Disorders

My Ebook Publishing House
Bucharest, 2020

TABLE OF CONTENTS

INTRODUCTION

Mental illness has been recognized in people dating back to days of Ancient Greece and Rome. A number of disturbances that were described included feelings of melancholy, hysteria and phobias. The concept that mental illness must be related to biology was first considered by Hippocrates. While at this time serious conditions such as schizophrenia were not yet recognized, the thought that these conditions were related to the brain was there.

As time passed, several psychiatric theories developed and even crude treatments were developed to treat individuals. Many of these treatments and theories for mental illness were developed by Islamic medicine in the Middle East. One of the most notable doctors of the 8th Century who was noted for his theories and treatments was the physician Rhazes of the Baghdad Hospital.

At the start of the 20th Century, there were only about a dozen officially recognized conditions, but by 1952 nearly 192 conditions were known and today the *Diagnostic and Statistical Manual of Mental Disorders, Fourth Edition* (DSM-IV) lists 374.

This eBook is designed to provide you with a guide to various mental illnesses and to assist you in understanding the various diagnosis and mental health problems that are common today. You will also find many remedies to assist you in supporting individuals who suffer from these conditions.

Disclaimer: This information provided here is not presented by a medical practitioner and is for educational and informational purposes only. The content is not intended to be a substitute for professional medical advice, diagnosis or treatment. Always seek the advice of your physician or other qualified health care provider with any questions you may have regarding a medical condition. Never disregard medical advice or delay in seeking medical assistance because of something you have read.

Since natural and dietary supplements are not FDA approved they must be accompanied by a two-part disclaimer on the product label that the statement has not be evaluated by the FDA and that the product is not intended to "diagnose, treat, cure or prevent any disease."

CHAPTER 1

UNDERSTANDING MENTAL ILLNESS
AND DIAGNOSIS

Many people are confused by mental illness and many will claim that they simply do not exist, that the condition is caused by the person experiencing it. However, everyday there are counselors who are diagnosing people as having mental illness conditions and because of this it makes it difficult to determine whether or not a diagnosis is correct.

Also, because of this, there are many controversies surrounding these conditions.

Mental health is essential for everyday life. Most people are able to go through life without any glitches in their mental process, but others seem to have constant interruptions. It is these interruptions that show us that there is something going wrong in the brain of these individuals and that there is an existing problem.

We need to look at different diagnoses and symptoms to understand the interruptions that occur in the brain. For example, we should take bipolar depression as an example. This is one of the most common disorders diagnosed in today's society. In fact, you probably know somebody with bipolar depression you just don't know that they have it. Bipolar is very common, but many people don't fully understand the condition. Bipolar is a chemical imbalance in the brain. This means that the brain is denied of vital nutrients that it needs to maintain a stable mindset. The problem is that many people who are diagnosed with the condition do not have their full life experiences taken into consideration. We all experience stress, trauma and drama in our lives. However, not everybody deals with these stressors in the same manner as somebody else would and nobody should be expected to deal with these stressors in the same manner as someone else would. There is a process that takes place that brings on the condition of bipolar depression.

The first thing that you must consider is that we all have "triggers." These triggers are the stressful events that happen in life. Now, everybody deals with these differently.

Some people will respond negatively and others ignore. Those individuals who ignore these issues are often not hearing the messages in between. This is what separates the mentally ill mind from the "normal" mind. The mentally ill mind tends to absorb everything in life that is said. The hear it all and they let all of that process in their brains until it begins to cause confusion. The "normal" mind tends to only listen to what it wants to listen to and therefore they do not have these conflicting thoughts to cause the mental confusion. To better understand this process, it helps to also understand cognitive mental health disorders and how these are related to the confusion that occurs in the mind.

Cognitive Mental Health Disorders

Cognitive health disorders include:

- Dementia
- Delirium
- Alcohol-induced disorders

There are also several others that are related and all of these are constantly being studied so that we may gain a better understanding of them. Most of these disorders have several common denominators such as loss of memory. Others are linked brain and biological disease, such as alcoholism and drug addiction. Often people who suffer from cognitive disorders have issues with reasoning and often their speech. They tend to lack good judgment and their comprehension is different from the "normal" mind.

These individuals also tend to suffer from another conditions such as:

- Depression
- Irritation
- Paranoia

There are several other related symptoms that are easily misdiagnosed with other conditions, such as bipolar, as bipolar condition encompasses several of these symptoms as well.

Delirium is one that is often confused because it includes:

- Signals confusion
- Speech problems
- Loss of memory
- Fear
- Depression

Many of these same symptoms are apparent in other mental illnesses, but delirium also has several physical effects on the body as well such as:

- Increased heart rate
- Nausea
- Disturbance in sleep

All of these physical symptoms as well as the mental confusion cause the person to not be able to find comfort in their life. Many studies have shown that medications can increase their symptoms as well to the point that the physical symptoms express themselves in strokes and heart attacks.

Dementia is a type of Alzheimer's disease. This causes the person to have issues with memory retention as well as learning and language. There are several physical conditions that can cause the onset of dementia such as AIDS, strokes, heart failures and other chronic conditions. People that suffer from dementia also tend to suffer in personal hygiene and poor judgment as well. They tend to avoid others, alter their personality and have social anxiety in general. Many are manic depressive and should completely avoid alcohol. Mentally ill patients tend to resort to drugs and alcohol and this only increases the symptoms of their condition and makes it worse, although it provides them temporary relief from their pain and suffering. However, alcohol and drugs are not a solution to anything in life and should be completely avoided by these individuals, as they are not likely to be able to keep their drinking at a social level.

There are alcohol induced disorders that have been classified as cognitive disorders because of the similar symptoms. In most of these cases the condition is a direct result of the condition, although this is not true of all individuals. Many individuals who are mentally ill have never touched drugs and alcohol, although many therapists will try to use alcohol and drugs as a reason for their condition. Those disorders that are alcohol induced are referred to as "Korsakoff's Syndrome" and it main affects the memory directly. Symptoms of this condition include:

- Memory loss
- Denial
- Indifferences
- Violent behaviors

Most of these conditions can be directly linked to nutritional deficiencies because the alcoholic and drug user tend to not live very healthy and eat poorly. Alcoholism is difficult to treat, but it is possible. However, it does require a lot of diligence by the patient and they must accept that they have a problem in order for recovery to occur. There are medications and treatments that can be used to assist the person and many will need therapy with high dosages of B-complex vitamins. If the patient is still in the early stages of alcoholism it will be easier to treat them as long as they are willing.

Alcoholism is a very serious condition and it even affects children.

Therapists are constantly looking for new ways to treat mental illness. There are millions of individuals around the world who suffer from mental illnesses and many rarely receive the care that they should.

The Roots of Mental Health Issues

There are several different types of mental illnesses and all have a root that prompts them to manifest somewhere in a person's life. There are various conditions that people may suffer from including:

- Adjustment disorders
- Bipolar
- Sexual disorders
- Dementia
- Delirium
- Manic Depression

Adjustment disorders are common when a person has a hard time adapting to stress in their life. Bipolar is another common disorder that is often diagnosed in individuals, but this condition can easily be misconstrued and can be misdiagnosed. Bipolar or manic depression affects individuals and often includes symptoms such as:

- Hyperactivity
- Excessive worrying
- Mood swings

These individuals seem to go from extreme highs to extreme lows in just a matter of minutes. They can literally drive a person crazy if they are not treatedimmediately.

These individuals often threaten suicide, although many are just looking for attention and never actually attempt suicide. This condition is directly linked to a chemical imbalance in the brain and the condition is more neurological than physiological. This condition also has been linked to genetics and is likely to be passed on in a family.

Many patients that have been diagnosed have a family history of similar behavior and mood swings. Many of these chemical disorders are often linked back to childhood development and trauma that the person sustained and never received treatment for. If the trauma is allowed to fester and the person never has to accept and deal with it, bipolar symptoms will occur.

Sexual disorders also occur in a similar way. These disorders are separate from bipolar and other adjustment disorders. Sexual deviation is often linked to abuse, although not always, pornography, and other types of negative sexual behaviors. Recent studies have proven, however, that serial killers and sociopath behaviors are hereditary. Some studies have linked these conditions to child abuse and this may be the case in some instances, but not necessary all instances. Sexual disorders are psychological and there have been links of brain impairments that cause interruptions in the brain's processes which cause this behavior to manifest itself.

Dementia and delirium are mind disorders that tend to manifest themselves in older individuals. These cause memory loss and confusion. These can be tricky to diagnose if the patient is young as the condition could be caused by other illnesses in young individuals.

What You Should Ask a Mental Health Expert

If you or a family member or friend is in therapy there are questions you should ask to avoid problems. The expertise level of therapists do vary and not all are qualified to diagnose mental illness. If you suspect that you have a disorder you should do your best to be very accurate on your symptoms, research them and document them. If you go to a therapist you will be ahead of the game and by knowing and researching your symptoms you may be able to prevent an incorrect diagnosis.

When you visit a therapist they will talk to you and listen to you. They will search for many signs and disturbances in your thinking patterns. Therapists will search for symptoms such as:

- Vague thoughts
- Fleeting ideas
- Peripheral thought patterns
- Blocking thoughts
- Disassociation
- Break in reality
- Paranoia

If the patient displays a disturbance in their thinking patterns, the therapist may consider psychosis. Counselors will consider schizophrenia or psychosis if the patient shows a break in reality. Paranoid and paranoia may be misconstrued if the therapist doesn't have a good understanding between the two conditions. Schizophrenics are often paranoid and may suffer from posttraumatic stress in the early stages. If a patient provides answers to questions that are unrelated, the therapist may consider a potential mental illness. Another area of concern is if the patient speaks in fragments of thoughts and don't deliver complete sentences or ideas. This is known as a fleeting thought process. If a patient is illustrating thoughts that are off the subject, the therapist may also show concern.

Other areas that are considered include language. Some patients may simply have a lack of education, but they should be able to speak in a comprehensible manner. It is important that the patient is not misdiagnosed simply because they have poor communication skills. Because every person is different and may have a different level of education it is important that that the therapist pay attention to symptoms that are linked to mental health. Be certain to ask the therapist questions any time there is a diagnosis and what the diagnosis is based on. For example, if the patient is telling the therapist about a dream and all of a sudden can't remember what they are talking about, this can be an evident that the patient has suffered trauma. The symptoms are in front of the therapist, but it is wise to continue therapy to verify the diagnosis.

Many therapists are not trained sufficiently in certain conditions, such as Multiple Personality Disorder. These conditions require you to carefully examine the person because they may only be suffering from dementia. However, if they are suffering from Multiple Personality Disorder it is often because they are trying to block traumatic memories to avoid pain.

It is always wise to ask questions when you are visiting a therapist and this can also help them to avoid any mistakes. A healthy mind is important and mental health should not be taken lightly. Therapists are constantly studying the mind and often use the guinea pig method until they figure out what the issue is. Mental health symptoms are serious and should not be taken lightly.

CHAPTER 2

COMMON MENTAL ILLNESSES

There are several mental illnesses and scientists are constantly searching to understand the various mental illnesses that exist. Here we will discover just a few of the most common illnesses in detail.

Alcohol Abuse and Drug Abuse

Alcohol abuse and drug abuse are two conditions that are both very serious. However, it seems that alcoholism often gets more attention than drug abuse, when drug abuse should often be looked at more closely. The DSM manual suggests that there are actually differences in the definition of both conditions. To confuse matters even more, the judicial system seems to have its own version of what these conditions are as well.

Some of the most common symptoms of alcoholism and drug abuse include:

- Excessive drinking/drugging
- Problems with the law
- Withdrawal symptoms
- Shaking of hands

If a person drinks daily and relies on alcohol, then you are most likely dealing with an alcoholic. Although, everyone seems to have their own definition of what an alcohol is, but the bottom line is that withdrawal symptoms manifest themselves and the person needs alcohol to relieve them then they are an alcoholic, no matter what time of the day they have their first drink.

Each person is different physically in how they deal with alcohol as well. If you are started drinking when you were young and you have been able to drink without alcohol causing you any issues then you are probably not an alcoholic. The fact is that alcoholism and drug addiction are very complex conditions. Alcohol and drugs become a problem when the person is unable to control their use and increases their intake and then combines the two. If someone will steal or lie to obtain alcohol then they are likely addicted. Many people with other mental illnesses will also resort to alcohol and drugs to find relief from their symptoms.

Alcoholism and drug addiction are conditions that can be treated and overcome but it does require a lot of motivation to quit on the person's behalf. Many people must first hit rock bottom before they are willing to admit that they have a problem and many people are never able to admit they have a problem and there is little hope for these individuals. You can't make a person quit drinking or doing drugs, but you can support them once they have taken it upon themselves to quit.

Antisocial and Psychopathic Disorders

To diagnose antisocial and psychopathic disorders, mental health experts first use the Conduct Control Behaviors or Disorders rules to diagnose a patient over the age of 18 with Antisocial Personality Disorder. This particular disorder often has several underlying disorders that can mimic other symptoms to cause a false diagnosis. These symptoms may include, but are not limited to:

- Fire starting and pyromania
- Truancy
- Theft

- Harming of people
- Harming and killing small animals
- Hostility towards authority
- Violent outbursts
- Dangerous sexual acts
- Willful or malicious destruction of property
- Compulsive-implosive explosions
- Crime

There are many more symptoms related to this condition, but quite frankly many are very frightening.

Psychopathic symptoms are very similar to those above and include:

- Fire starting
- Bed wetting
- Harming or killing people
- Harming or killing small animals
- Explosive outbursts
- Conduct control disorders
- Inability to regard others
- Destruction
- Truancy
- Neglectful attitude

- Sexual deviant behavior
- Hostility towards authority
- Inability to show remorse
- Inability to express emotions
- Impulsive-compulsive behaviors
- Criminal minded

Individuals who suffer from antisocial and psychopathic conditions are unable to show emotion at all and they never show remorse for their actions. If they do show remorse, it is superficial and they really don't have any feelings of remorse at all. These two areas of mental illness include the following illnesses:

- Antisocial personalities
- Sociopath personalities
- Histrionic personalities
- Psychopathic personalities

It is easy to see how these conditions can have a similar diagnosis, as they are related and linked quite closely in diagnosis. The differences are slight and in reality the two are very similar. These two conditions are often diagnosed and linked to each other in a condition called Psychopathic disorder with Antisocial Personality Disorder, Psychopathic traits and tendencies. Because of the closeness in diagnosis, many mental health experts have conflicting opinions on Antisocial Personality Disorder, because it is essentially psychopathic. Psychopathic Personalities are up on reality, but their morals and social beliefs tend to determine their symptoms. These people often engage in sexual exploits and are more often affected by pornographic materials and pornographic materials are often the leading cause behind a psychopath's mind.

These conditions also have hereditary link and their behaviors are genetic. Also, although alcohol and drug use are common among these individuals, not all are alcoholics or drug addicts. Several individuals have been diagnosed with this condition and have never touched either substance. Many resort to these substances though to relieve the pain of their symptoms.

These individuals do not always commit murder either. Many of those who do commit murder are those who have not been treated. It may take years to work through the symptoms of these conditions, but in the long run you can work with them and treat them. This is important to stop these individuals from becoming serial killers. It is often the individuals who are never treated that resort to killing.

Auditory Processing Hyperactive Disorder (ADHD)

Auditory Processing Hyperactive Disorder is also known as Attention-Deficit Hyperactivity Disorder or better yet, ADHD. ADHD is a product of the misprocessing of the auditory stimuli and a hearing deficiency. Auditory Processing Hyperactive Disorder is coupled with Attention Deficit and Hypertension Disorder. Auditory Processing Hyperactive Disorder is most common in children and teenagers and not so much in adults. However, adults have recently been diagnosed quite frequently as of late.

Warning signs of this condition include:

- Incapacity to use common sense
- Verbalizes without caring about others
- Constantly feeling a great sense of boredom
- Lack of focus
- Act before thinking
- Disregard the consequences of their actions and behaviors

The cranial nerve that connects the inner ear with the brain transfers impulses that control balance and hearing. When the auditory process is interrupted, the person feel aggravated and becomes hyperactive. This leads to Attention Deficit Hyperactivity.

These individuals seem to have an unyielding amount of energy and they often act out inappropriately.

Recent studies have also shown us that the central nervous system plays a large role in the functioning of learning and coping skills. Researchers have also found this condition to be associated with the neurotransmitter deficiency ailment. The neurotransmitter process is associated with the central nervous system and problems then become noticeable. If this can be treated then the disorder may be treated as well because they are linked.

Diet may play a large role in this condition as well. Most patients who are diagnosed often lack in a healthy diet. Parents are advised to contact a professional if their child exhibits these behaviors and they will look at your child's diet with you to ensure they are receiving the proper nutrients for a healthy central nervous system. The patient who is not diagnosed may become suicidal.

ADHD is common in children and many of these children will resort to drugs and alcohol to relieve themselves of their symptoms. If your child is suspected of suffering from this condition then they should receive proper treatment and therapy.

You also need to ensure the diet is not deficient in any nutrients as this does have an effect. Many children will require a good diet plan, therapy, natural supplements, and chiropractic tactics.

Avoidant Personality Disorder

Avoidant Personality Disorder is a personality type that will avoid the public due to a fear of rejection, disappointment, humiliation, and that people will view them as a failure. They are often reluctant to speak in public, ask for help or ask questions.

These individuals also tend to work below their abilities, as being promoted is frightening to them. Many of these individuals will also suffer from:

- Inferiority complexes
- Severe episodes of loneliness
- Depression
- Anxiety attacks

Schizoid personality types are similar to this condition; however, they will avoid public but still need to socialize. Avoidant Personality Disorder types do not have a desire to socialize at all.

Avoidant personality types are easy to treat without medication because their symptoms are all rooted in fear. Therapeutic treatment can work through their fears by starting with the deepest fear the person displays. Through talk therapy, role play and other strategies, therapists can do wonders for avoidant personality disorders. It is important to listen to these types, as the problem lies in their thoughts andconcerns.

When a person is telling someone that they have a problem with socialization, we know that underneath those words lies fear that is often caused by an incident or accident from their childhood. These individuals may have endured some underdevelopment or lack of education and knowledge as well because they stay under the radar in an attempt to not out perform others. If this person is taught or relearns the rules of society they can often socialize without problems. If a therapist can work through the problems without covering them up with medication then the person can come out of their shell.

Dependent Personality Disorder

Dependent Personality Disorders are common according to many mental health experts. These individuals suffer from symptoms such as:

- Incompetence to make their own decisions

- Rely on others to make decisions for them

- Avoid responsibility

- Rely on others to handle their lives and tasks

- Avoid tasks unless someone else guides them through the process.

- Tolerate abuse and neglect, including the cheating of a spouse

- Often depressed

- Often abuse alcohol and drugs to relieve anxiety

- Passive

- Will not defend themselves

- Afraid of rejection

- Afraid of punishment

It is important that these symptoms are carefully scrutinized and they should not be confused with women who are submissive, as the traditional woman will not tolerate anyone going against their beliefs and will defend their person without thinking twice.

Dependent personality types are found in individuals who have Histrionic and Borderline personality types. The difference is that Histrionic and Borderline personality types may be manipulative, controlling, abusive and act out dangerously. These individuals can be manipulative and may even murder. The dependent personality type is not aggressive and can hold a relationship, while Histrionic and Borderline personality types cannot hold a relationship.

Dependent personality types need ongoing therapy because they have underlying fear from undo punishment, neglect or abuse. The person most likely lived in an unruly home and received harsh punishment. Most dependent types will rely on their parents to make their decisions for them and the parent often finds a reason to dismiss the decisions the person does make. For example, if the person was engaged in a relationship that broke up, the parent will tell them something like, "I told you so, that girl/boy was too good for you." They are constantly put down as not being able to make good decisions for themselves, so they rely on others to do it for them. These individuals will become so dependent that they begin to ask for permission for anything they do, even simple tasks like going to bed or going to the store.

These people become co-dependent because their parents won't allow them to move forward in life. Therefore, the patient must separate him or herself so that they begin to develop their own independence. Therapists must also use techniques that will
34

work to help the patient separate from those that they are dependent upon and move towards relying on themselves. Most therapists will rely on talk therapy because the patient holds the answers, they just don't realize it because they are used to being told that they are wrong. In most instances we know that the patient was neglected or harshly punished often and often scolded. It is also useful to work through their mental problems. You can talk through their problems and sort out the information to gather the background of the person's behavior. While working with these individuals the therapist should never raise their voice r attempt to control them. They must be allowed to speak freely and open up. Do not allow the person to blame his or herself as this only contributes to their dependency.

Schizophrenia

Schizophrenia is a condition that has plagued the mental health world for decades. Mental health experts have been finding more cases of these individuals than they have in the past. This condition is nothing that should be ignored and ignoring the diagnosis only adds to the problem. Schizophrenia has several levels of symptoms and these patients must be treated immediately. Any person complaining of any of the following must receive treatment immediately:

- Paranoia
- Hallucinations
- Hearing voices

These individuals suffer immensely and those around them also suffer because of the person's actions and lack of reality. They often feel that someone is trying to get them or coming to get them. They may also tell you that the CIA or KGB is out to get them as well.

Hallucinations affect the sensory in the sense that it conveys messages to sense organs and then creates a suspicious force. This causes the person to be suspicious of everything around them including objects, places, things and people. Once they suspicion sets in they can become extremely dangerous and may act out violently.

The twin area of the brain is affected in this condition and causes the individual to break off from reality. Medication is often required to prevent schizophrenic episodes and hallucinations.

Researchers have been astounded by this condition for years and are always seeking answers to questions regarding the condition. The hallucinations that these individuals suffer from are similar to psychotic breaks and the patient looses contact with reality. The voices that they hear often tell them that there is danger near, which is often not true. An example of a serious schizophrenic was the Oklahoma City Bomber.

Signs that a person may be schizophrenic include:

- Laughing for no apparent reason
- Shouting at the air
- Constant muttering during periodicals
- Covering ears

Most individuals who suffer from this condition are recognized by the age of 13 and these individuals are often not treated until later in life when they should be treated much earlier. This is often because certain symptoms are often found in other disorders and professionals wait to see if the person is a true schizophrenic or if they are suffering from another condition.

The downside is that if the person is not treated early enough they often break into paranoia and this is when diagnosis is quite dangerous. The reason is because they begin to hear voices in their head and they may claim the voices are from God, the Devil or aliens. Their visual perspective is often similar to the voices they hear in their head. They may tell you that they see people from the CIA or KGB or that someone delivered packages to their door, etc.

These individuals are not typically suicidal, but would rather kill than die. There have been a few cases of schizophrenics showing suicidal behaviors however.

Impulsive Behaviors

Impulse Control Disorders are becoming more common in today's children. There are few people who have never acted on an impulse, but when symptoms are reoccurring and consistent then the individual needs help. Judgment plays a large role in impulses and if the judgment is ignored in a dangerous situation someone may get hurt. Most of the individuals suffering from this condition act on impulses against their better judgment. In many cases these behaviors hurt others.

These individuals also tend to not have the ability to regard the law, society, him or herself or others. They simply act without thinking. The patient also has an intense feeling to act out on an impulse even though his instinct says "no."

Intermittent Explosive Disorder is the worst of these conditions because the end result can be deadly if left untreated.

These individuals illustrate explosive behaviors and patients with this disorder have neurological and brain aberrations. Many of these individuals are very dangerous and other mental illnesses are often lurking beneath the surface.

For example, a child could be diagnosed with Intermittent Explosive Disorders, Impulsive Control Disorder, Antisocial Disorder, Oppositional Defiance and Psychopathic Tendencies. These individuals can be hard to treat and many will tell you there is no treatment for them. These individuals will do several dangerous acts including:

- Abuse a person to the point of death
- Bash walls
- Bust windows
- Terrorize the home
- Hurt animals
- Start fires
- Make explosives
- Engage in pornographic materials obsessively
- Laugh for no reason
- Walk around with a deranged look

This is also just the beginning of their actions in many ways. These individuals will also show no remorse for their actions and may even blackout during their explosions.

These individuals also appear to have a good side and an evil side. They tend to be triggered by certain actions or words, but they may also explode for no apparent reason. Founding counseling for these individuals is often difficult if you can find them at all. Many will simply tell you that it is hereditary and there is nothing they can do for you. Parents can deal with these children by showing absolutely no fear for them and using reverse psychology.

Impulse Control Disorders also include Pathological Gambling Obsessions. This activity is often uncontrollable as well once the addiction of gambling sets in. These people may also have underlying disorders such as:

- Antisocial personalities
- Mood swings
- Alcohol and drug addiction
- Depression
- OCD

These individuals also resort to theft and kleptomania.

Pyromaniacs are also placed in this category because they are unable to control their impulses. These individuals set fires and watch them burn. They will also extend this beyond their own home. These people have issues with substance abuse, self-esteem, resist authority and other similar symptoms. If you notice someone sitting around and burning items in the home and laughing about it you will want to watch this person closely. Some individuals only show slight symptoms while others will be moresevere.

Multiple Personality Disorder and Posttraumatic Stress

These two conditions are often linked together because the person may develop additional personalities to deal with their stress. These patients are often the survivors of severe abuse. Multiple Personality Disorders often have several symptoms including:

- Distinct personalities
- Personalities of different genders
- Personalities of different ages
- Multiple signatures
- Different IQs
- Personality Types

- Amnesia
- Voices in the head
- Frequent nightmares
- The use of "we" when referring to self
- Outer body experiences

These patients are often alone in the world because the experts do not usually have enough information to understand their diagnosis. It is often difficult to ever hear the truth about these conditions as well. These patients will often fight against lying and will strive for accuracy. Female patients are rarely violent, while males may be. Some males patients have been sent to prison for crimes including robbery and rape.

Patients often act on projection or interjection caused by an alter personality. This condition has been questioned as whether or not it is real, but the fact is that it is a true condition. Many have tried to pretend to have multiple personalities to get out of crimes by way of insanity, but it is nearly impossible for these individuals to maintain distinct personalities.

Personalities may include child alters, teens, adults and even elderly personalities. All personalities are a sub part of the actual person who has been traumatized to the point that they are no longer able to cope. These individuals are also very intelligent. These individuals tend to have issues and difficulty with medical treatment as their blood pressure may raise and lower, they may have seizures and their respiratory rates may change. Some personalities may even be blind.

The patient often goes through life with the disorder and when they reach a certain age they have no chance of coping. This is when integration of the personalities needs to occur. Integration places the alter personalities in an area of the mind to stay permanently. Once the integration is complete, these individuals may have a hard time going back to normal life as they have lived most of their life with their "family" in their mind. These individuals have a sense of loss because they don't know how to cope in the world without their personalities. It is possible for the personalities to communicate with each other after integration, but it is never the same. Many individuals have a difficult time going through life because they are used to the daily stress of work and life being shared by their other personalities and now they only have themselves to depend on.

Dangerous Personality Disorders

There are several types of personality disorders. Some we have already discussed and others we have mentioned. Now we talk about the various other disorders that have been alluded to and are often combined with other mental illnesses.

Borderline Personality Disorder

Borderline Personality Disorder symptoms include:
- Impulsive behaviors
- Mood swings that are unpredictable
- Terrified of being abandoned
- Promiscuous behaviors
- Manipulation
- Self-destructive behavior
- Violence behavior

It is possible to treat these individuals but they can be dangerous to live with. These individuals may cut themselves to seek attention and may even threaten suicide. They tend to offer a love/hate relationship and will seek similar characteristics in other individuals. Other symptoms may include short-term psychotic breaks, illicit behaviors, depression, demanding behaviors and denial. This disorder is linked to incest, emotional breakdowns in families and alcoholism and drug addiction.

Histrionic Personality Types

These types often act and will play the role of the victim in most situations. These individuals may display the following:

- Vanity
- Narcissism
- Anger
- Seductive
- Flirty
- Extreme violence to the point of murder

These individuals may be diagnosed with other illnesses as well.

Obsessive Compulsive Disorders

These conditions are known by their behaviors. These people tend to display the following:

- Disregard for rules and regulations
- Perfectionists
- Inability to complete tasks
- Controlling with one type of person, such as less authority figures

- Acts out of self-control around authority figures to hid their identity

- Views people as objects

This type is common and are often domestically violent individuals. These individuals often have the problem of completing tasks because they are not very flexible people and disregard other feelings and emotions. These patients tend to abuse others that show emotion to them.

All of the personality types listed above tend to have a look of seriousness at all times. They may force themselves to laugh around others. All of these personality types tend to be dangerous as they do not have any feelings for others. Many of the individuals who commit homicides suffer from one of the following:

- Antisocial Personality Disorder
- Borderline Personality Disorder
- Histrionic Personality Disorder
- OCD – it is reported that these individuals kill slowly
- Psychopathic
- Sociopath
- Schizophrenia

These individuals are difficult to treat and in some cases impossible if the person refuses to accept help.

Underdeveloped Child Separation

Many emotional breakdowns are caused by individuals who have not separated from their inner person at childhood. Many mental illnesses in society are complicated because we do not always see to the root of the problem. The child within exists throughout our lifetime and if we do not recognize this "inner child" we tend to suffer from emotional breakdowns. As a result, many professionals struggle to find a way to treat patients with this disorder.

Many of these people were ignored as children and were emotionally neglected and maybe even physically abuse and many have witnessed bad scenes in life that haunt them. Unless the problems are dealt with the issue continues to grow. To contact the inner self the person has to have a basic knowledge of their problem. Once a basic knowledge is situation, the person is then able to move on to the next step.

Once a person has basic understanding of themselves they are able to move forward with the help of therapy. Many diagnoses stem from brain injuries, chemical and physical imbalances. Effective treatment is not always possible until the person is able to deal with their problems.

For example, a schizophrenic was once found to have a disease of the mind because the twin holes of the brain had a larger side to the cavity of the brain. This condition is also genetic and many of these people have disruptive childhoods and will often deny that happenings occurred. As long as the patient is in denial, it is difficult to impossible to treat them.

Another example can also be seen when patients are diagnosed with posttraumatic stress disorder. These patients were also subjected to trauma in their childhood and the disorder escalates during that experience. The solution for this is to address the child beneath the disorder and then move forward to treat the trigger of the disorder. Once you dig deep enough you will be able to help the patient become acquainted with the child within and then treat the patient more effectively.

Many people have difficulty treating these disorders because they do not completely listen to the patient. Many therapists have the idea of they are holding the degree so they know more than the patient does. If more people listened then this would not be such an issue in society. The best solution begins with listening to the patient and actually hearing what they are saying. These individuals often have to take things one day at a time as well.

Passive Aggressive Disorders

Passive-Aggressive Personality types often sabotage various areas of their life in the sense that they complain about demands that are put on them. They may not voice their complaints but they are cussing them out in their minds and the person or thing that made them do the work.

Passive-Aggressive types are exactly as the name implies. They are often passive outwards, but aggressive inwards. These people often anger others around them, yet the person may feel wrong for not being clear on the foundation that caused the anger. These types of people are also deceiving as they use obscure tactics in persecuting others.

For example, say Troy confronts Kelly expressing to him that her behaviors were wrong and that they were causing problems. Kelly looks at Troy with a glare tells Kelly that he is the problem. Kelly says she did what she was supposed to and that he did nothing wrong that Troy doesn't know what he's talking about.

This disorder often causes controversy and is often disputed, but the term is used frequently.

Self-Defeating Personality Disorders often associate with person that will cause harm to persecute the person or self-defeat them. This person will also excuse another person's offer to help them even if the help is needed. This type of person may also anger others around them and then display hurt when they are confronted. These two personality types are not able to hold permanent relationships in most cases and will make excuses for their behavior.

Sadistic Personality Disorders were recently removed from the DSM manual because of a lack of foundation for diagnosis. The symptoms included not being able to control their behavior. These people are violent and will harm others to uphold control over another person. This disorder is similar to psychopathic and antisocial personality disorders and may rejoice when they hurt other people or animals. Even if the person is submissive, the person will often torture or hurt others because it gives them pleasure. Persons that suffer from this disorder are often survivors of abuse and are angry at the world around them. These individuals cannot typically maintain a relationship and will hurt the person involved in their life.

CONCLUSION

Relating to others with mental illness can be difficult. If you have a mental illness then the only people who often understand you may be your therapist or doctor and even those people will sometimes fail. Many patients will complain that their therapist is not helping them and they will complain about the medication and treatment they receive. The problem is that there is a communication breakdown between the two people and patients do not always do their best to follow instructions and listen to their therapist.

Often when a patient complains there is a reason and something is not working somewhere. It is important that if the patient is complaining of voices or hallucinations telling them things, you must listen to them as they can become dangerous.

Do not simply push it away and call them crazy. You will often have to read between the lines with patients. It is important that they are understood and that they are listened to so that you can help them cope with their problems and symptoms.

Printed by Libri Plureos GmbH in Hamburg,
Germany